Cookies

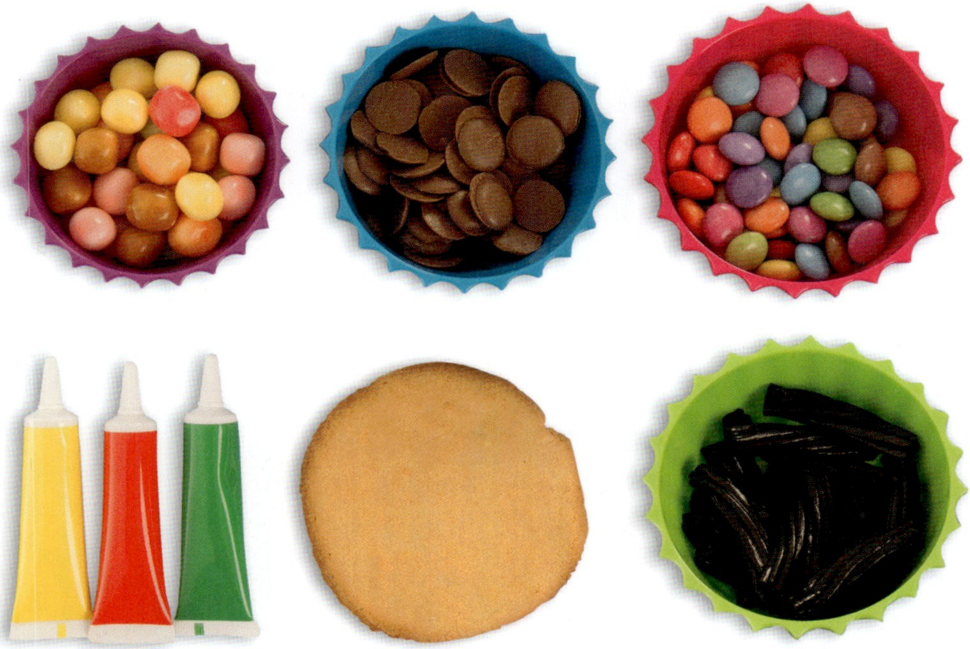

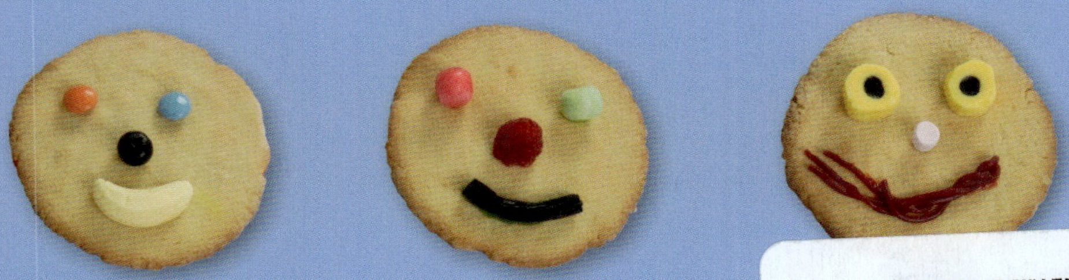

Written by Marie Layson-Dale
Illustrated by Beatrice Costamagna

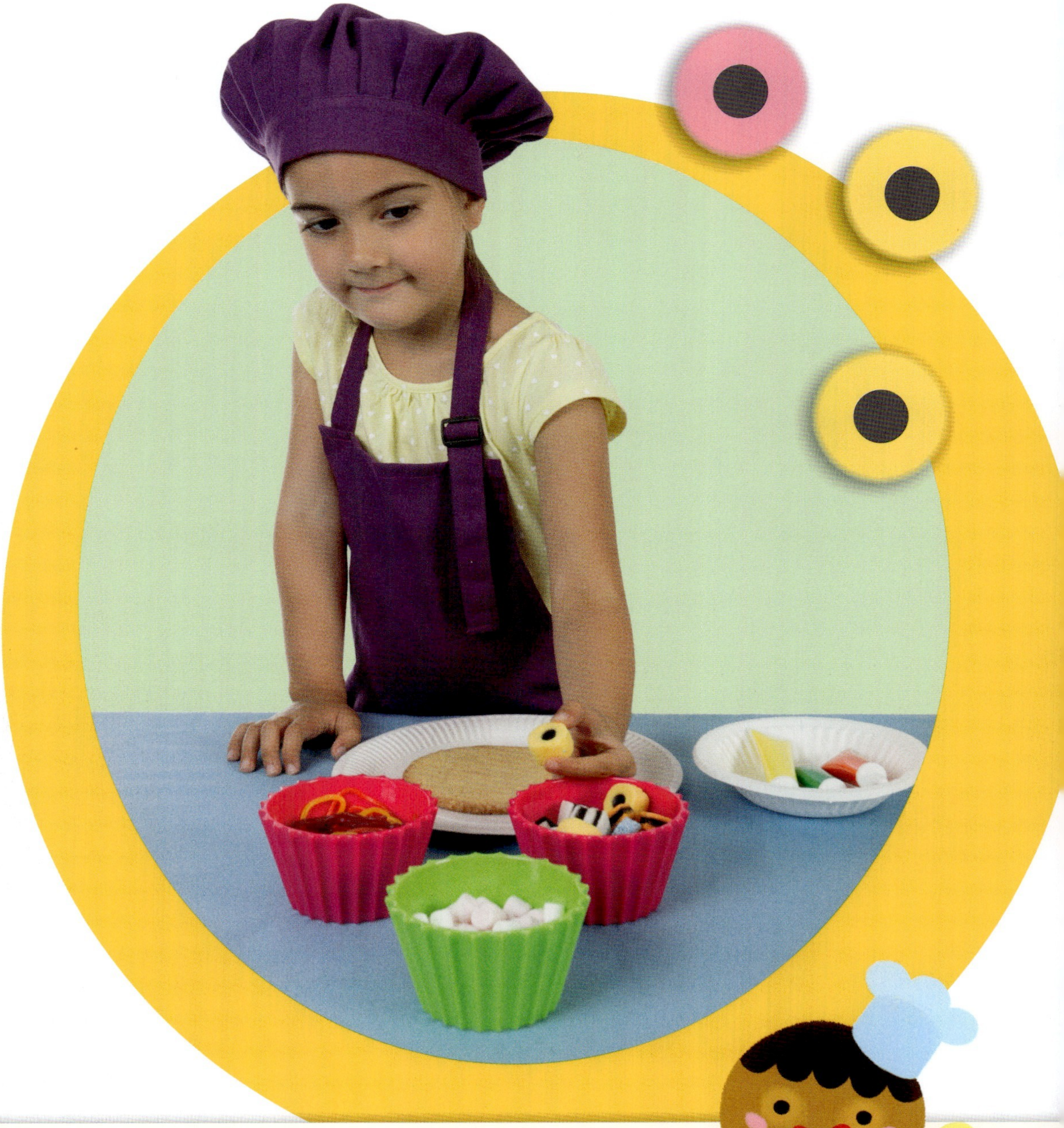

Pick the eyes.

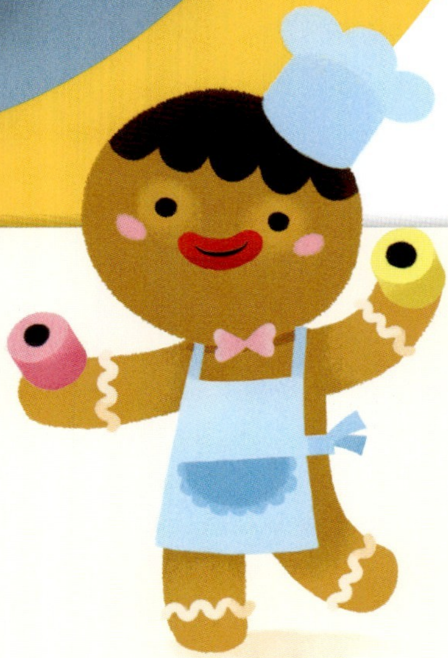

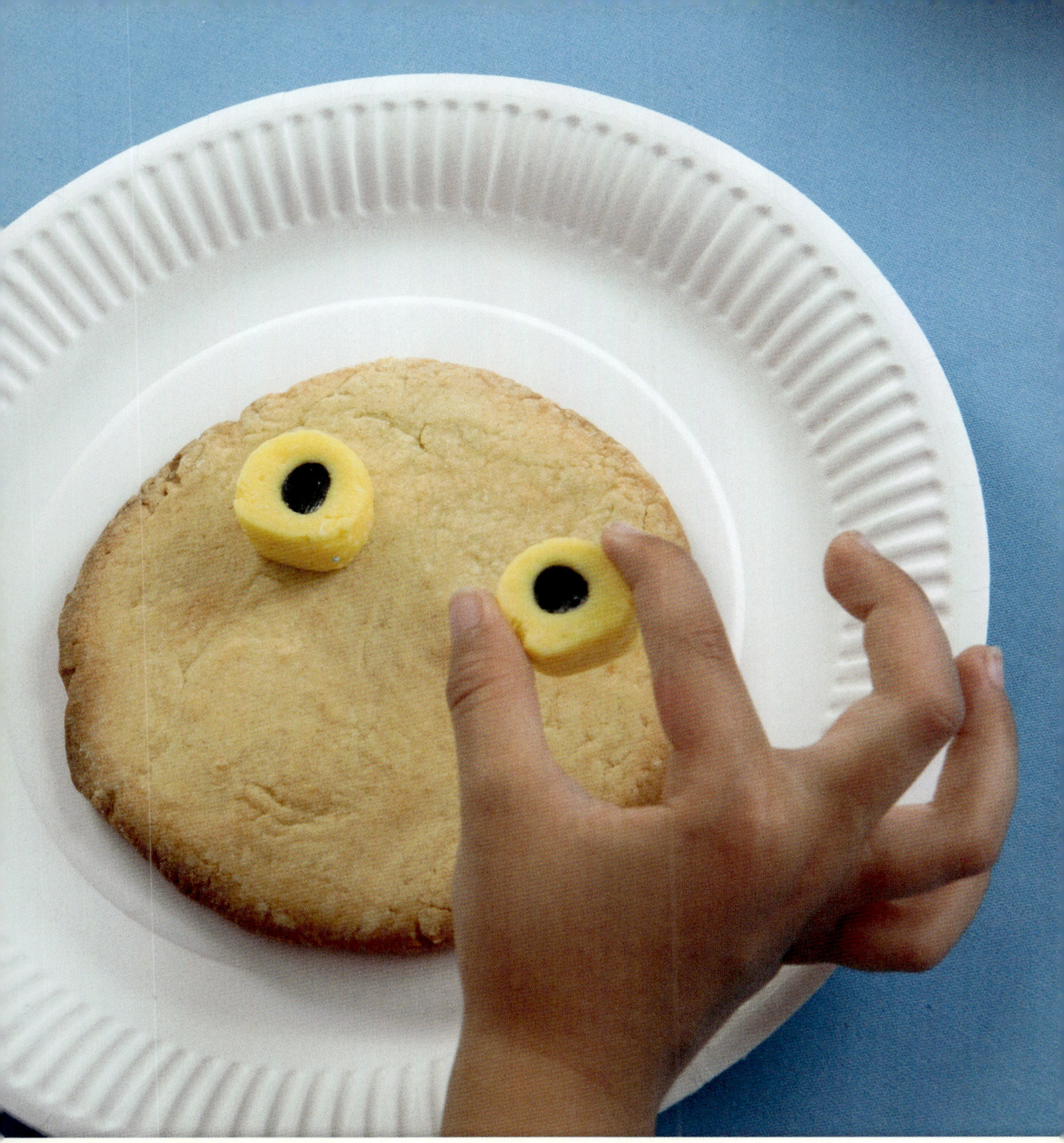

Pop the eyes on.

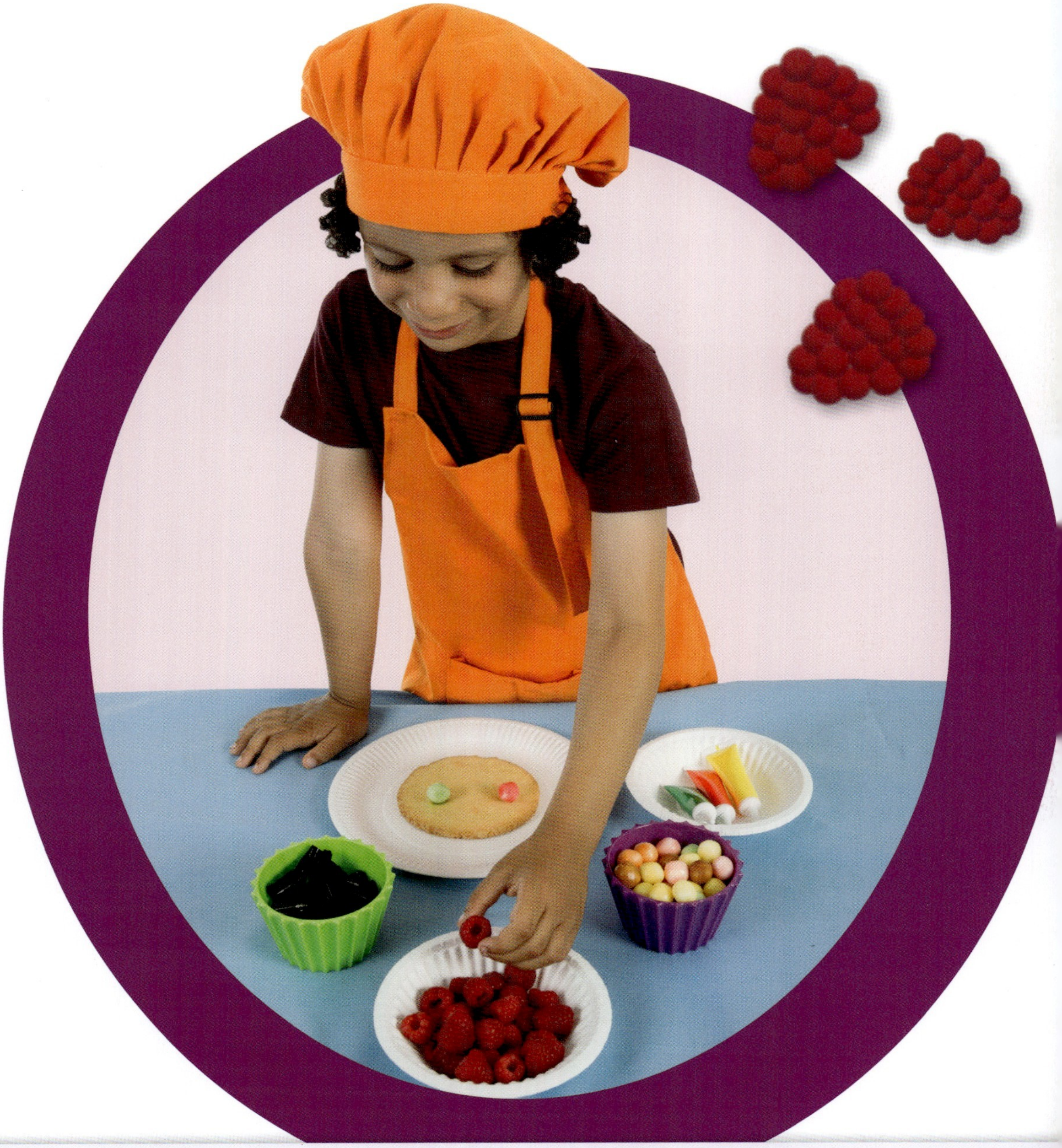

Pick the nose.

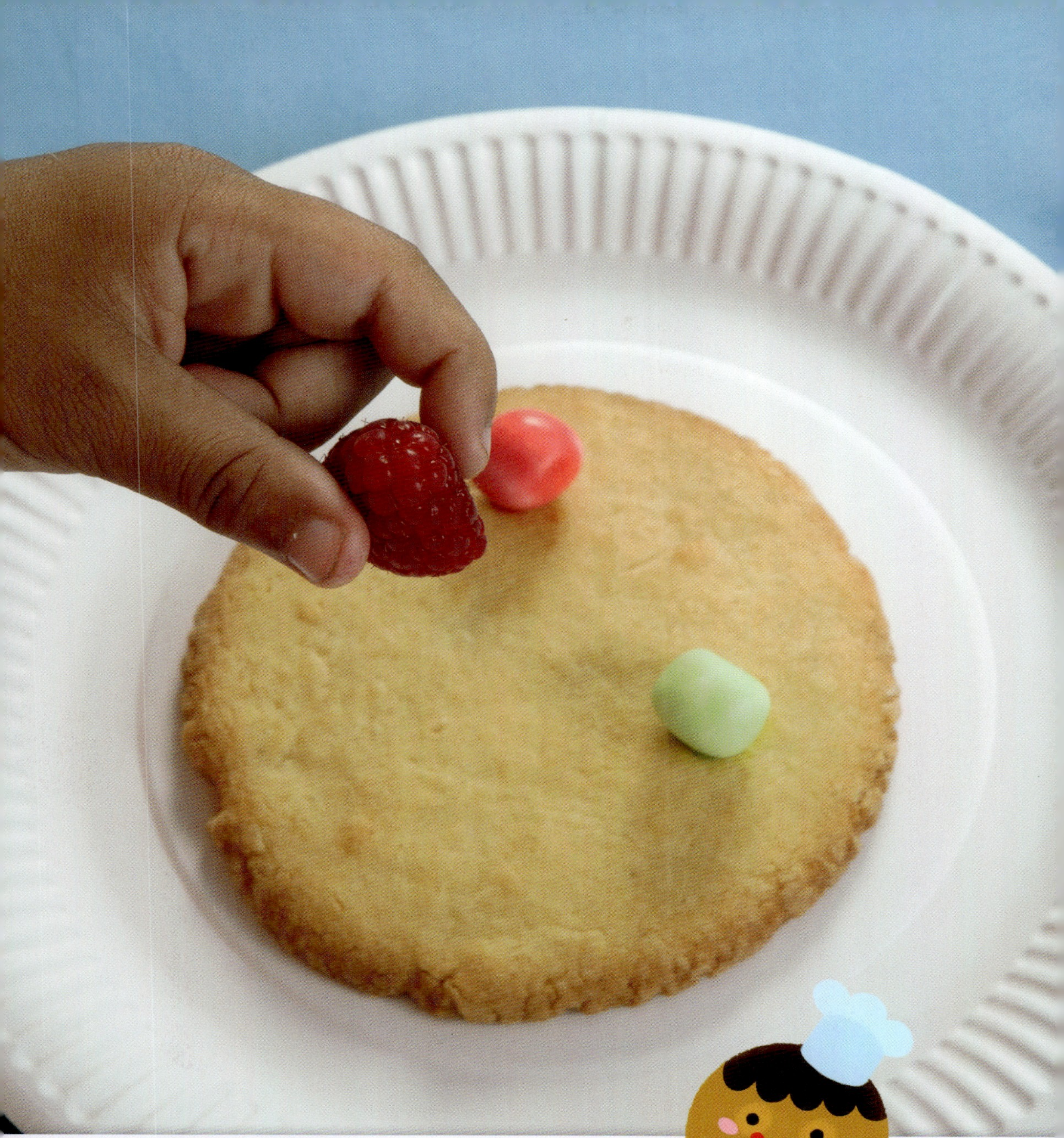

Pop the nose on.

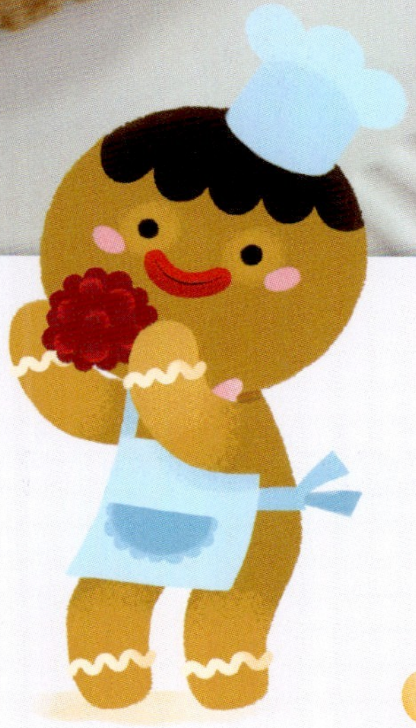

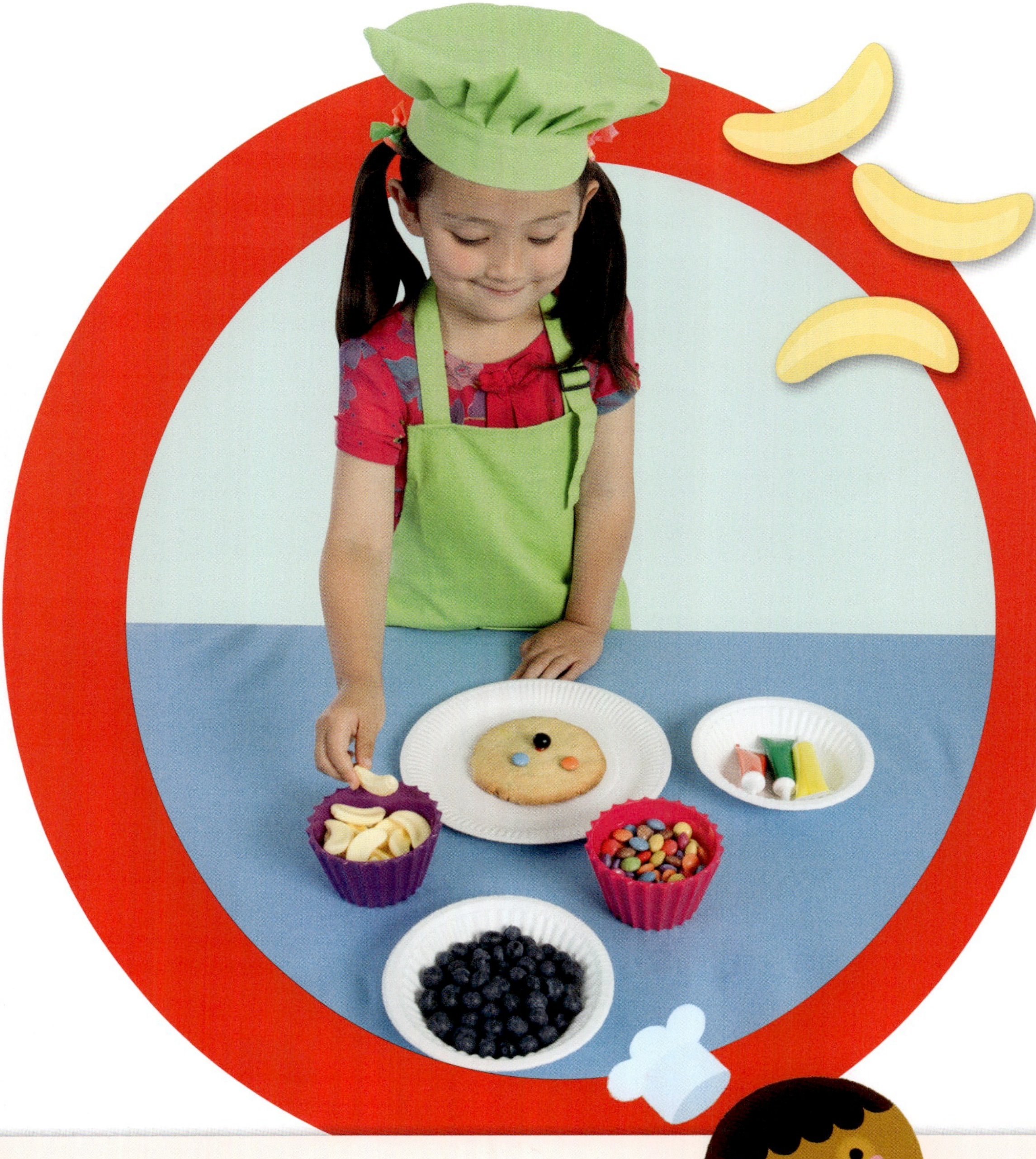

Pick the mouth.

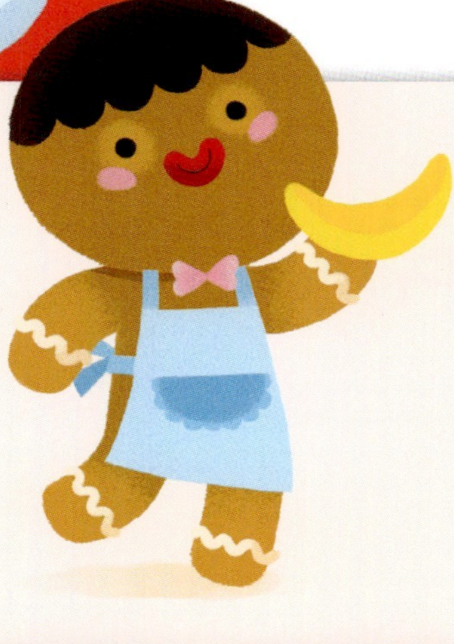

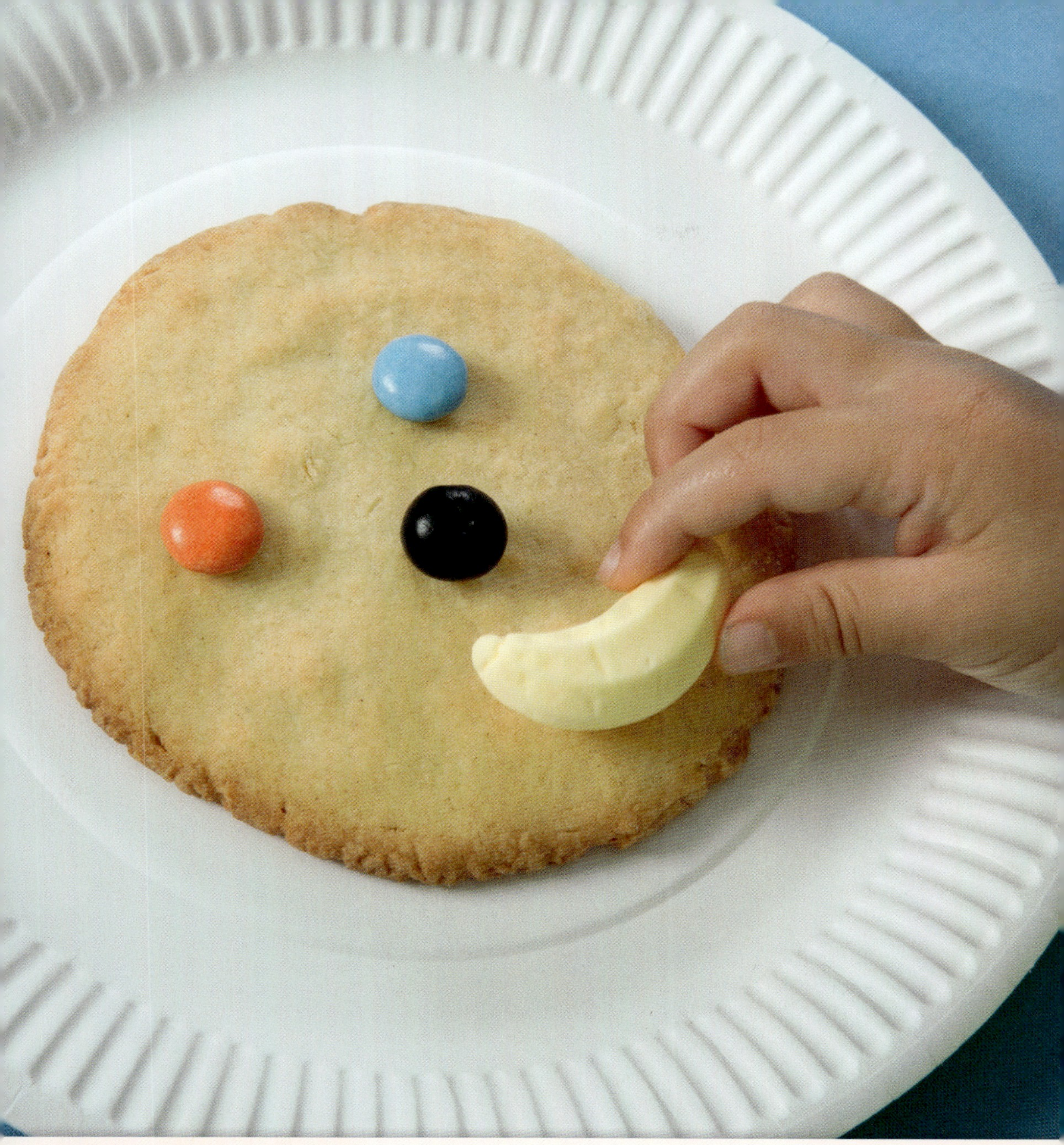

Pop the mouth on.

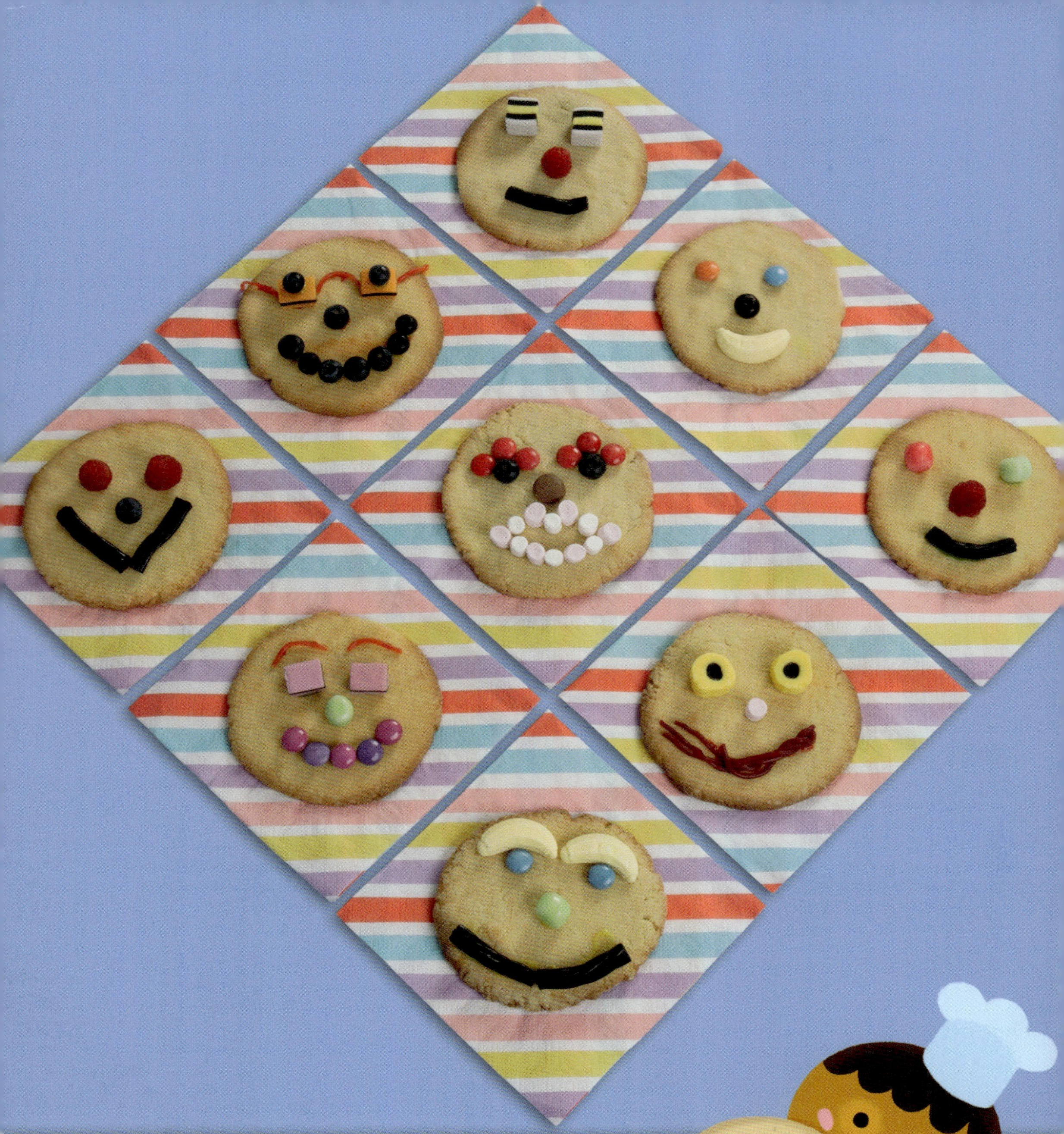

Pick the cookie!

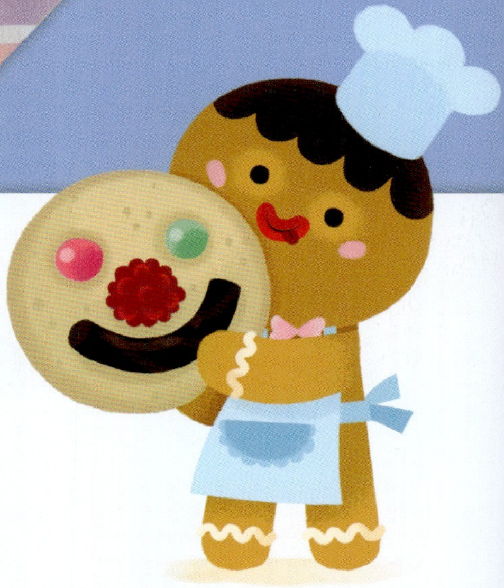